Of A Woman
Willetta

Copyright ©2013 by Willetta Davis

To Mama

and all the survivors and fighters of breast cancer.

La Nueva Puntada
1401 E. Crawler
Irving, Texas 75061
(214) 596-1673

Server: **Anahi**   Station: 5

Order #: 1196439   Take Out

》 SETTLED 《

Taco Mañanero	10.50
huevo con papa	
extra condimento	0.25
extra condimento	0.25
guacamole chico	3.00
SUB TOTAL:	14.00
Tax 1:	0.91
TOTAL:	**$14.91**
Cash Tendered:	20.00
CHANGE:	-5.09

》 Ticket #: 69 《
Created: 7/14/2018 8:45:44 AM
SETTLED: 7/14/2018 8:46:23 AM

THANK YOU!

La Hacienda
1401 ... ...
Irving, Texas ...
(214) 556-1674

Server: Andy   Station: 5

Opr: 1196529   Dine In

>> STUFF <<

Taco Madness	0.50
Huevo con Papa	
ex tra condimento	2.25
ex tra cooztepec	0.25
enchilade phila ?	.00

TOTAL $10.91

Tender Cash   20.00

CHANGE: 9.09

>> Ticket Info <<
Opened 07/09/2015 6:50:54 AM
Printed 07/09/2015 6:58:47 AM

THANK YOU!

Who can find a virtuous woman? For her price is far above rubies.

Proverbs 31:10

Her Presence

When they see me coming they all move aside

As I pass through I see admiration and adoration in their eyes

I hear the wondering in their voices asking

Who am I?

Where did I come from?

Where have I been?

After my presence they ask

Have you seen her?

Will we see her again?

Her Spirit

I have many names

I wear many faces

I've seen many things

I've been many places

I'm adorned in the spirit

I am laced with dignity and pride

I'm as prayerful as Hannah

As graceful as Esther

As pure as Mary

In my heart is where truth lies

In my mouth there are words of wisdom

My tongue only speak words of kindness

To my husband I am virtuous

My children rise up and call me blessed

Her Honor

I am respected and greeted by

Madame, Miss, Ms. and Mrs.

I am the Prince's bride

I am Queen

Queen to my King

Queen of the land

I am Mother

Mother of love

Mother of nature

Mother of Abraham, Isaac, Jacob, Moses and Jesus

I am God's greatest creation to bear great men

Her Nurturing Nature

I am blessed with giving

My bosom carries the milk that nurtures many nations

My fingertips are numb from the grinding of the grains

These hands prepare many meals and clothed many who are naked

My womb carries the fruit where I bear daughters and sons

Her Song & Praise

I'm exalted in the book of Ruth

Praised in Proverbs

And even Solomon has song me a Song

I am the sunshine on cloudy days

When it's hot, warm, or cold outside

I'm the months of January, February, March, April, and May

June, July, August, September, October, November and December

I'm always in your thoughts

Never forgotten always remembered

Her Wisdom

I am the mother of the Civil Rights Movement

I am the Queen of Soul

I am the other half of man that makes man whole

I am young

I am old

I am wise

I am bold

I 'm always right

Never wrong or so I'm told

Her Beauty

Many call me beautiful

Yet, I'm not vain

Though they adorn my feet with rose petals

It's to God I give the highest praise

I am highly favored

But I'm not deceitful

Nikki says I'm Ego Tripping

But Maya says I'm Phenomenal

Her Dignity

I am full of respect

Therefore I'm respectful

I will never be disrespected

Because I am respectable

Many have tried to belittle me beat me and break me

But I am unbreakable

Her Value

I am far more precious than rubies

Far more valuable than diamonds, silver, or gold

I wear the finest of garments

Not of satin or silk

But strength and honor are how I'm clothed

Her Strength

Men and children there is something I want you to know

When you are weak

I am strong

and

When you slip

I am your backbone

Her Name

I've been many places

I've seen many things

I wear many faces

And I have many names

Mother, Ma'Dear, Mama, Big Mama, Lil' Mama,

Sweetie, Sister, Auntie, Baby, Girl,

Honey, Chil', Lady, Pearl

Her Character

I'm a strong, loving, caring, understanding one

I'm Black, White, Native American, Hispanic,

Middle Eastern, Indian, Asian, African…

Her Purpose

I've been in this world since time began

Placed my mark in stone and sand

Became a mother to a motherless child

Taught the unlearned and nursed a sad heart into a smile

Sailed on the Nile

And…

I even slept in the Garden of Eden for a little while

Her Beginnings

You see...

*In the beginning God created and image of Him
and called him man*

and

Named him Adam

And as he slept I was created

Flesh of his flesh

Bones of his bones

And when Adam awakened

He took one look at me

Named me Eve

And called me...

Her Glory

"Woman"!

To God be the Glory for giving me these words of inspiration

Our Prayer

Thank you Lord for this blessed day
Lead us in the path of righteousness
As we walk along the way
Guide us Lord
So we won't stray
Give us strength to conquer dismay
Protect us Jesus each and everyday
With these and many blessings we ask
In Jesus name
We pray
Amen

Copyright ©2013 by Willetta Davis

Made in the USA
San Bernardino, CA
04 May 2018